GOD IS A MAN

ERNEST MUHAMMAD

ISBN: 978-0-578-56837-9

AMAZON.COM OR LULU.COM

My Email Address: godisaman2020@gmail.com

If you feel that this book is the truth and good for Black folks, show some love, take a photo of the book or make a short video and put it on social media.

Thank You,

Gracias

非常感谢你

- *Ernest Muhammad*

Point No. 12
Of The
Muslim Program

What the Muslims Believe

WE BELIEVE that Allah (God) appeared in the Person of Master W. Fard Muhammad, July, 1930; the long-awaited "Messiah" of the Christians and the "Mahdi" of the Muslims.

We believe further and lastly that Allah is God and besides HIM there is no god and He will bring about a universal government of peace wherein we all can live in peace together.

I thank Allah for the man who gave me actual facts on the reality of God coming in the person of a man. The Hon. Minister Louis Farrakhan.

What Is Logical thinking?

Logical thinking is the process in which one uses reasoning consistently to come to a conclusion. Problems or situations that involve logical thinking call for structure, for relationships between <u>facts</u>, and for chains of reasoning that "make sense."

Jeremiah 1:9 (KJV)

Then <u>**the LORD**</u> **put forth** <u>**his hand,**</u> **and** <u>**touched my mouth.**</u> <u>**And the LORD said unto me**</u>**, Behold,** <u>**I**</u> **have put** <u>**my**</u> **words in thy mouth.**

Matthew 5:8 (KJV)

Blessed are the pure in heart:

for they shall <u>see God</u>.

Genesis 5:24 (KJV)

And Enoch <u>walked with God</u>.

Definition of Speak

Speak:

(1) <u>Say something</u> in order to convey information, an opinion, or a feeling.

(2) <u>Communicate</u> in or be able to communicate in (<u>a specified language</u>)

(3) <u>Talk</u> to in order to give or extract information.

(4) Mention or discuss <u>with speech</u>.

(5) <u>Talk</u> to in order to reprove or advise.

**Grade level for knowing what the word "speak" means:
3rd grade**

Example of God talking

Exodus 33:11 King James Version

And the LORD spake unto Moses **face to face,** as a man speaketh unto his friend.

Spake:

Simple past tense of ***speak****.*

Said:

(1) Past and past participle of say.

(2) Utter words so as to convey information, an opinion, a feeling or intention, or an instruction.

Grade level for knowing what the word "said" means: 3rd grade

Face:

The front part of the <u>head</u>, from the <u>forehead</u> to the <u>chin</u>.

Grade level for knowing what the word "face" means: 2nd grade

Hear:

(1) Perceive <u>with the ear</u> the sound made by (someone or something).

(2) Listen to all that someone has to say.

(3) Be aware of; know of the existence of.

Walking:

(1) Move at a regular pace by lifting and setting down each <u>foot</u> in turn, never having both <u>feet</u> off the ground at once.

(2) To move along on <u>foot</u> : advance by steps

Example:

Genesis 3:8 (KJV)

And they <u>heard</u> the <u>voice</u> of the LORD <u>God</u> <u>walking</u> in the garden in the cool of the day: and Adam and his wife hid themselves from the <u>presence</u> of the LORD God amongst the trees of the garden.

Grade level for knowing what the word "person" means:
3rd grade

Grade level for knowing what the word "foot" means:
1st grade

Grade level for knowing what the word "walking" means:
3rd grade

Grade level for knowing what the word "voice" means:
3rd grade

Personal Pronouns

A personal pronoun is a word that is used as a substitute for the <u>proper name of a person.</u> *I, you, he, she, it, we they, me, him, her, us,* and *them* are all personal pronouns.

<u>Personal:</u>

Relating or belonging to
<u>a single or particular person</u> rather than to a group or an organization:

In referring to God, does your Pastor or Minister ever use the personal pronouns He, Him or His?

**Grade level for knowing what a personal pronoun is:
4th grade**

The Word "He" In Arabic

(هو) – Huwa – pronoun

Meaning

<u>He</u> (when referring to the <u>male human</u>)

A Very Important Example

Holy Quran - Sura (Chapter) 112

***In the name of Allah, the Beneficent, the
Merciful.***

112:1 Say: <u>He</u>, Allah, is One.
112:2 Allah is <u>He</u> on Whom all depend.
112:3 <u>He</u> begets not, nor is <u>He</u> begotten;
112:4 And none is like <u>Him</u>.

Examples:

Exodus 6:29 That **the LORD spake** unto Moses, saying, **I** *am* the LORD: speak thou unto Pharaoh king of Egypt all that **I** say unto thee.

Exodus 8:1 And **the LORD spake** unto Moses, Go unto Pharaoh, and say unto him, Thus saith the LORD, Let my people go, that they may serve **me.**

Grade level for knowing if you say "I" or "ME," it's talking about a person, not a ghost:
3rd grade

Genesis 1 (KJV)

And God said, Let us make man in our image, after our likeness: and let them have dominion over the fish of the sea, and over the fowl of the air, and over the cattle, and over all the earth, and over every creeping thing that creepeth upon the earth. So God created man in his own image, in the image of God created he him; male and female created he them.

Grade level for knowing that a ghost (spirit) can't have an image:
3rd grade

How Speech is Produced

Speech production is the process by which <u>thoughts</u> are translated into **speech**. ...
Normally **speech** is created with pulmonary pressure <u>provided by the lungs</u> that generates sound by phonation through the glottis in the larynx that then is modified by the vocal tract into different vowels and consonants.

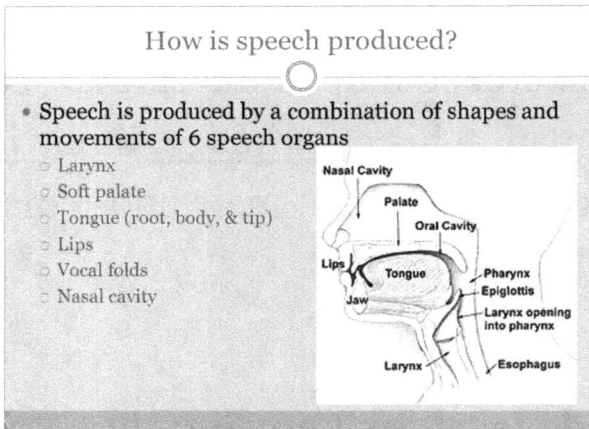

How is speech produced?

• Speech is produced by a combination of shapes and movements of 6 speech organs
  - Larynx
  - Soft palate
  - Tongue (root, body, & tip)
  - Lips
  - Vocal folds
  - Nasal cavity

Nasal Cavity
Palate
Oral Cavity
Lips
Tongue
Jaw
Pharynx
Epiglottis
Larynx opening into pharynx
Larynx
Esophagus

Does a spook (spirit or holy ghost) God have lungs?

If you answered yes to this, please go to Page 150.

The Lord (God) Talks

Exodus 6:10 <u>And **the LORD spake**</u> unto Moses, <u>saying,</u>

Exodus 6:13 <u>And **the LORD spake**</u> unto Moses and unto Aaron, and gave them a charge unto the children of Israel, and unto Pharaoh king of Egypt, to bring the children of Israel out of the land of Egypt.

Exodus 6:28 And it came to pass on the day *when* <u>**the LORD spake**</u> unto Moses in the land of Egypt,

Exodus 7:8 <u>And **the LORD spake**</u> unto Moses and unto Aaron, saying,

Exodus 7:19 <u>And **the LORD**</u>
<u>spake</u> unto Moses, Say unto Aaron, Take thy
rod, and stretch out thine hand upon the
waters of Egypt, upon their streams, upon
their rivers, and upon their ponds, and upon
all their pools of water, that they may become
blood; and *that* there may be blood
throughout all the land of Egypt, both
in *vessels of* wood, and in *vessels of* stone.

Numbers 1:1 <u>And **the LORD**</u>
<u>spake</u> <u>unto Moses</u> in the wilderness of Sinai,
in the tabernacle of the congregation, on the
first *day* of the second month, in the second
year after they were come out of the land of
Egypt, saying,

Numbers 20:12 <u>And **the LORD spake** unto Moses and Aaron</u>, Because ye believed <u>me</u> not, to sanctify <u>me</u> in the eyes of the children of Israel, therefore ye shall not bring this congregation into the land which <u>I</u> have given them.

Numbers 20:23 <u>And **the LORD spake** unto Moses and Aaron</u> in mount Hor, by the coast of the land of Edom, saying,

Numbers 21:16 And from thence *they went* to Beer: that *is* the well **<u>whereof the LORD spake</u>** unto Moses, Gather the people together, and <u>I</u> will give them water.

Deuteronomy 4:15 Take ye therefore good heed unto yourselves; for ye saw no manner of similitude on the day *that* **the LORD spake** unto you in Horeb out of the midst of the fire:

Deuteronomy 5:22 These words **the LORD spake** unto all your assembly in the mount out of the midst of the fire, of the cloud, and of the thick darkness, with a great voice: and he added no more. And he wrote them in two tables of stone, and delivered them unto me.

Deuteronomy 9:10 And the LORD delivered unto me two tables of stone written with the finger of God; and on them *was written* according to all the words, which **the LORD spake** with you in the mount out of the midst of the fire in the day of the assembly.

Deuteronomy 9:13 <u>Furthermore **the LORD spake** unto me, saying, I</u> have seen this people, and, behold, it *is* a stiffnecked people:

Deuteronomy 10:4 And he wrote on the tables, according to the first writing, the ten commandments, which <u>**the LORD spake**</u> unto you in the mount out of the midst of the fire in the day of the assembly: and the LORD gave them unto me.

Joshua 1:1 Now after the death of Moses the servant of the LORD it came to pass, that <u>**the LORD spake** unto Joshua the son of Nun, Moses' minister, saying,</u>

Joshua 4:1 And it came to pass, when all the people were clean passed over Jordan, that <u>**the LORD spake** unto Joshua, saying,</u>

Joshua 4:8 And the children of Israel did so as Joshua commanded, and took up twelve stones out of the midst of Jordan, as **the LORD spake** unto Joshua, according to the number of the tribes of the children of Israel, and carried them over with them unto the place where they lodged, and laid them down there.

Joshua 4:15 And **the LORD spake** unto Joshua, saying,

Joshua 14:10 And now, behold, the LORD hath kept me alive, as he said, these forty and five years, even since **the LORD spake** this word unto Moses, while the children of Israel wandered in the wilderness: and now, lo, I am this day fourscore and five years old.

Joshua 14:12 Now therefore give me this mountain, <u>whereof **the LORD spake** in that day;</u> for thou heardest in that day how the Anakims were there, and that the cities were great and fenced: if so be the LORD will be with me, then I shall be able to drive them out,<u> as the LORD said.</u>

Judges 2:4 And it came to pass, when the angel of **the LORD spake** these words unto all the children of Israel, that the people lifted up their voice, and wept.

1 Kings 5:5 And, behold, I purpose to build an house unto the name of the LORD my God, as **the LORD spake** unto David my father, saying, Thy son, whom I will set upon thy throne in thy room, he shall build an house unto my name.

1 Kings 12:15 Wherefore the king hearkened not unto the people; for the cause was from the LORD, that he might perform his saying, which **the LORD spake** by Ahijah the Shilonite unto Jeroboam the son of Nebat.

2 Kings 10:10 Know now that there shall fall unto the earth nothing of the word of the LORD, which **the LORD spake** concerning the house of Ahab: for the LORD hath done *that* which he spake by his servant Elijah.

2 Kings 21:10 And **the LORD spake** by his servants the prophets, saying,

1 Chronicles 21:9 And **the LORD spake** unto Gad, David's seer, saying,

2 Chronicles 33:10 And **the LORD spake** to Manasseh, and to his people: but they would not hearken.

Isaiah 7:10 Moreover **the LORD spake** again unto Ahaz, saying,

Isaiah 8:11 For **the LORD spake** thus to me with a strong hand, and instructed me that I should not walk in the way of this people, saying,

Jeremiah 30:4 And these *are* the words that **the LORD spake** concerning Israel and concerning Judah.

Jeremiah 46:13 The word that **the LORD spake** to Jeremiah the prophet, how Nebuchadrezzar king of Babylon should come *and* smite the land of Egypt.

Jeremiah 50:1 The word that **the LORD spake** against Babylon *and* against the land of the Chaldeans by Jeremiah the prophet.

Jonah 2:10 And **the LORD spake** unto the fish, and it vomited out Jonah upon the dry *land*.

Malachi 3:16 Then they that feared **the LORD spake** often one to another: and the LORD hearkened, and heard *it*, and a book of remembrance was written before him for them that feared the LORD, and that thought upon his name.

Exodus 33:11 And **the LORD spake** unto Moses face to face, as a man speaketh unto his friend. And he turned again into the camp: but his servant Joshua, the son of Nun, a young man, departed not out of the tabernacle.

Exodus 40:1 And **the LORD spake** unto Moses, saying,

Leviticus 4:1 <u>And **the LORD spake** unto Moses, saying,</u>

Leviticus 5:14 <u>And **the LORD spake** unto Moses, saying,</u>

Leviticus 6:1 <u>And **the LORD spake** unto Moses, saying,</u>

Leviticus 6:8 <u>And **the LORD spake** unto Moses, saying,</u>

Leviticus 6:19 <u>And **the LORD spake** unto Moses, saying,</u>

Leviticus 6:24 <u>And **the LORD spake** unto Moses, saying,</u>

Leviticus 7:22 <u>And **the LORD spake**</u> unto Moses, saying,

Leviticus 7:28 <u>And **the LORD spake**</u> unto Moses, saying,

Leviticus 8:1 <u>And **the LORD spake**</u> unto Moses, saying,

Leviticus 10:8 <u>And **the LORD spake**</u> unto Aaron, saying,

Genesis 1:3 <u>And **God said**</u>, Let there be light: and there was light.

Genesis 1:6 <u>And **God said**</u>, Let there be a firmament in the midst of the waters, and let it divide the waters from the waters.

Genesis 1:9 <u>And **God said**</u>, Let the waters under the heaven be gathered together unto one place, and let the dry *land* appear: and it was so.

Genesis 1:11 <u>And **God said**,</u> Let the earth bring forth grass, the herb yielding seed, *and* the fruit tree yielding fruit after his kind, whose seed *is* in itself, upon the earth: and it was so.

Genesis 1:14 <u>And **God said**</u>, Let there be lights in the firmament of the heaven to divide the day from the night; and let them be for signs, and for seasons, and for days, and years:

Genesis 1:20 <u>And **God said**</u>, Let the waters bring forth abundantly the moving creature that hath life, and fowl *that* may fly above the earth in the open firmament of heaven.

Genesis 1:24 <u>And **God said**</u>, Let the earth bring forth the living creature after his kind, cattle, and creeping thing, and beast of the earth after his kind: and it was so.

Genesis 1:26 <u>And **God said**</u>, Let <u>us</u> make man in <u>our</u> image, after our likeness: and let them have dominion over the fish of the sea, and over the fowl of the air, and over the cattle, and over all the earth, and over every creeping thing that creepeth upon the earth.

Genesis 1:28 And God blessed them, <u>and **God said** unto them</u>, Be fruitful, and multiply, and replenish the earth, and subdue it: and have dominion over the fish of the sea, and over the fowl of the air, and over every living thing that moveth upon the earth.

Genesis 1:29 <u>And **God said,**</u> Behold, I have given you every herb bearing seed, which *is* upon the face of all the earth, and every tree, in the which *is* the fruit of a tree yielding seed; to you it shall be for meat.

Genesis 2:18 <u>And the LORD **God said,**</u> *It is* not good that the man should be alone; I will make him an help meet for him.

Genesis 3:1 Now the serpent was more subtil than any beast of the field which the LORD God had made. And he said unto the woman, Yea, hath <u>**God said,**</u> Ye shall not eat of every tree of the garden?

Genesis 3:13 <u>And the LORD **God**</u> **said** <u>unto the woman</u>, What *is* this *that*thou hast done? And the woman said, The serpent beguiled me, and I did eat.

Genesis 3:14 <u>And the LORD **God**</u> **said** <u>unto the serpent,</u> Because thou hast done this, thou *art* cursed above all cattle, and above every beast of the field; upon thy belly shalt thou go, and dust shalt thou eat all the days of thy life:

Genesis 3:22 <u>And the LORD **God said**,</u> Behold, the man is become as one of <u>us,</u> to know good and evil: and now, lest he put forth his hand, and take also of the tree of life, and eat, and live for ever:

Genesis 6:13 <u>And **God said** unto Noah,</u> The end of all flesh is come before <u>me</u>; for the earth is filled with violence through them; and, behold, <u>I</u> will destroy them with the earth.

Genesis 9:12 <u>And **God said**,</u> This *is* the token of the covenant which I make between me and you and every living creature that *is* with you, for perpetual generations:

Genesis 9:17 <u>And **God said** unto Noah,</u> This *is* the token of the covenant, which <u>I</u> have established between me and all flesh that *is* upon the earth.

Genesis 17:9 <u>And **God said**</u> unto Abraham, Thou shalt keep <u>my</u> covenant therefore, thou, and thy seed after thee in their generations.

Genesis 17:15 <u>And **God said** unto Abraham,</u> As for Sarai thy wife, thou shalt not call her name Sarai, but Sarah *shall* her name *be*.

Genesis 17:19 <u>And **God said,**</u> Sarah thy wife shall bear thee a son indeed; and thou shalt call his name Isaac: and <u>I</u> will establish my covenant with him for an everlasting covenant, *and* with his seed after him.

Genesis 20:6 <u>And **God said**</u> unto him in a dream, Yea, <u>I</u> know that thou didst this in the integrity of thy heart; for <u>I</u> also withheld thee from sinning against me: therefore suffered <u>I</u> thee not to touch her.

Genesis 21:12 And **God said** unto Abraham, Let it not be grievous in thy sight because of the lad, and because of thy bondwoman; in all that Sarah hath said unto thee, hearken unto her voice; for in Isaac shall thy seed be called.

Genesis 35:1 And **God said** unto Jacob, Arise, go up to Bethel, and dwell there: and make there an altar unto God, that appeared unto thee when thou fleddest from the face of Esau thy brother.

Genesis 35:10 And **God said** unto him, Thy name *is* Jacob: thy name shall not be called any more Jacob, but Israel shall be thy name: and he called his name Israel.

Genesis 35:11 And **God said** unto him, I *am* God Almighty: be fruitful and multiply; a nation and a company of nations shall be of thee, and kings shall come out of thy loins;

Exodus 3:14 And **God said** unto Moses, I AM THAT I AM: and he said, Thus shalt thou say unto the children of Israel, I AM hath sent me unto you.

Exodus 3:15 And **God said** moreover unto Moses, Thus shalt thou say unto the children of Israel, The LORD God of your fathers, the God of Abraham, the God of Isaac, and the God of Jacob, hath sent me unto you: this *is* my name for ever, and this *is* my memorial unto all generations.

Exodus 13:17 And it came to pass, when Pharaoh had let the people go, that God led them not *through* the way of the land of the Philistines, although that *was* near; for <u>**God said**</u>, Lest peradventure the people repent when they see war, and they return to Egypt:

Numbers 22:12 <u>And **God said**</u> unto Balaam, Thou shalt not go with them; thou shalt not curse the people: for they *are* blessed.

Judges 6:20 And the angel of **God said** unto him, Take the flesh and the unleavened cakes, and lay *them* upon this rock, and pour out the broth. And he did so.

1 Kings 3:5 In Gibeon the LORD appeared to Solomon in a dream by night: and **God said**, Ask what I shall give thee.

1 Kings 3:11 <u>And **God said** unto him,</u> Because thou hast asked this thing, and hast not asked for thyself long life; neither hast asked riches for thyself, nor hast asked the life of thine enemies; but hast asked for thyself understanding to discern judgment;

1 Chronicles 11:2 And moreover in time past, even when Saul was king, thou *wast* he that leddest out and broughtest in Israel: <u>and the LORD thy **God said** unto thee,</u> Thou shalt feed my people Israel, and thou shalt be ruler over my people Israel.

1 Chronicles 14:14 Therefore David enquired again of God; <u>and **God said**unto him,</u> Go not up after them; turn away from them, and come upon them over against the mulberry trees.

1 Chronicles 28:3 <u>But **God said** unto me,</u> Thou shalt not build an house for my name, because thou *hast been* a man of war, and hast shed blood.

2 Chronicles 1:11 <u>And **God said** to Solomon,</u> Because this was in thine heart, and thou hast not asked riches, wealth, or honour, nor the life of thine enemies, neither yet hast asked long life; but hast asked wisdom and knowledge for thyself, that thou mayest judge my people, over whom <u>I</u> have made thee king:

Jonah 4:9 <u>And **God said** to Jonah,</u> Doest thou well to be angry for the gourd? And he said, I do well to be angry, *even* unto death.

Luke 12:20 <u>But **God said** unto him,</u> *Thou* fool, this night thy soul shall be required of thee: then whose shall those things be, which thou hast provided?

Genesis 4:6 <u>And the LORD said unto Cain,</u> Why art thou wroth? and why is thy countenance fallen?

Genesis 4:9 <u>And the LORD said unto Cain,</u> Where *is* Abel thy brother? And he said, I know not: *Am* I my brother's keeper?

Genesis 4:15 <u>And the LORD said unto him,</u> Therefore whosoever slayeth Cain, vengeance shall be taken on him sevenfold. And the LORD set a mark upon Cain, lest any finding him should kill him.

Genesis 6:3 <u>And the LORD said,</u> My spirit shall not always strive with man, for that he also *is* flesh: yet his days shall be an hundred and twenty years.

Genesis 6:7 <u>And the LORD said,</u> <u>I</u> will destroy man whom <u>I</u> have created from the face of the earth; both man, and beast, and the creeping thing, and the fowls of the air; for it repenteth me that <u>I</u> have made them.

Genesis 7:1 <u>And the LORD said</u> unto Noah, Come thou and all thy house into the ark; for thee have <u>I</u> seen righteous before me in this generation.

Genesis 8:21 <u>And the LORD smelled</u> a sweet savour; <u>and the LORD said</u> in <u>his heart, I</u> will not again curse the ground any more for man's sake; for the imagination of man's heart *is* evil from his youth; neither will <u>I</u> again smite any more every thing living, as <u>I</u> have done.

Genesis 11:6 <u>And the LORD said,</u> Behold, the people *is* one, and they have all one language; and this they begin to do: and now nothing will be restrained from them, which they have imagined to do.

Genesis 13:14 <u>And the LORD said unto Abram,</u> after that Lot was separated from him, Lift up now thine eyes, and look from the place where thou art northward, and southward, and eastward, and westward:

Genesis 16:11 And the angel of the LORD said unto her, Behold, thou *art*with child, and shalt bear a son, and shalt call his name Ishmael; because the LORD hath heard thy affliction.

Genesis 18:13 And the LORD said unto Abraham, Wherefore did Sarah laugh, saying, Shall I of a surety bear a child, which am old?

Genesis 18:17 And the LORD said, Shall I hide from Abraham that thing which I do;

Genesis 18:20 And the LORD said, Because the cry of Sodom and Gomorrah is great, and because their sin is very grievous;

Genesis 18:26 <u>And the LORD said, If I</u> find in Sodom fifty righteous within the city, then <u>I</u> will spare all the place for their sakes.

Genesis 25:23 <u>And the LORD said unto her,</u> Two nations *are* in thy womb, and two manner of people shall be separated from thy bowels; and *the one*people shall be stronger than *the other* people; and the elder shall serve the younger.

Genesis 31:3 <u>And the LORD said unto</u> <u>Jacob,</u> Return unto the land of thy fathers, and to thy kindred; and <u>I</u> will be with thee.

Exodus 3:7 <u>And the LORD said, I</u> have surely <u>seen</u> the affliction of my people which *are* in Egypt, and have heard their cry by reason of their taskmasters; for <u>I know</u> their sorrows;

Exodus 4:2 <u>And the LORD said unto him,</u> What *is* that in thine hand? And he said, A rod.

Exodus 4:4 <u>And the LORD said unto Moses,</u> Put forth thine hand, and take it by the tail. And he put forth his hand, and caught it, and it became a rod in his hand:

Exodus 4:6 <u>And the LORD said</u> furthermore unto him, Put now thine hand into thy bosom. And he put his hand into his bosom: and when he took it out, behold, his hand *was* leprous as snow.

Exodus 4:11 <u>And the LORD said unto him,</u> Who hath made man's mouth? or who maketh the dumb, or deaf, or the seeing, or the blind? have not <u>I the LORD</u>?

Exodus 4:19 <u>And the LORD said unto Moses </u>in Midian, Go, return into Egypt: for all the men are dead which sought thy life.

Exodus 4:21 <u>And the LORD said unto Moses,</u> When thou goest to return into Egypt, see that thou do all those wonders before Pharaoh, which <u>I</u> have put in thine hand: but <u>I</u> will harden his heart, that he shall not let the people go.

Exodus 4:27 <u>And the LORD said to Aaron,</u> Go into the wilderness to meet Moses. And he went, and met him in the mount of God, and kissed him.

Exodus 6:1 <u>Then the LORD said unto Moses,</u> Now shalt thou see what <u>I</u> will do to Pharaoh: for with a strong hand shall he let them go, and with a strong hand shall he drive them out of his land.

Exodus 6:26 These *are* that Aaron and Moses,<u> to whom the LORD said,</u> Bring out the children of Israel from the land of Egypt according to their armies.

Exodus 7:1 <u>And the LORD said unto Moses,</u> See, <u>I</u> have made thee a god to Pharaoh: and Aaron thy brother shall be thy prophet.

Exodus 7:14 <u>And the LORD said</u> unto Moses, Pharaoh's heart *is* hardened, he refuseth to let the people go.

Exodus 8:16 And the LORD said unto Moses, Say unto Aaron, Stretch out thy rod, and smite the dust of the land, that it may become lice throughout all the land of Egypt.

Exodus 8:20 And the LORD said unto Moses, Rise up early in the morning, and stand before Pharaoh; lo, he cometh forth to the water; and say unto him, Thus saith the LORD, Let my people go, that they may serve me.

Exodus 9:1 Then the LORD said unto Moses, Go in unto Pharaoh, and tell him, Thus saith the LORD God of the Hebrews, Let my people go, that they may serve me.

Exodus 9:8 <u>And the LORD said unto Moses and unto Aaron,</u> Take to you handfuls of ashes of the furnace, and let Moses sprinkle it toward the heaven in the sight of Pharaoh.

Exodus 9:13 <u>And the LORD said unto Moses,</u> Rise up early in the morning, and stand before Pharaoh, and say unto him, Thus saith the LORD God of the Hebrews, Let my people go, that they may serve <u>me.</u>

Exodus 9:22 <u>And the LORD said unto Moses,</u> Stretch forth thine hand toward heaven, that there may be hail in all the land of Egypt, upon man, and upon beast, and upon every herb of the field, throughout the land of Egypt.

Exodus 10:1 <u>And the LORD said</u> unto Moses, Go in unto Pharaoh: for <u>I</u> have hardened his heart, and the heart of his servants, that I might shew these my signs before him:

Exodus 10:12 <u>And the LORD said unto Moses,</u> Stretch out thine hand over the land of Egypt for the locusts, that they may come up upon the land of Egypt, and eat every herb of the land, *even* all that the hail hath left.

Exodus 10:21 <u>And the LORD said unto Moses,</u> Stretch out thine hand toward heaven, that there may be darkness over the land of Egypt, even darkness *which*may be felt.

Exodus 11:1 <u>And the LORD said unto Moses,</u> Yet will <u>I</u> bring one plague *more*upon Pharaoh, and upon Egypt; afterwards he will let you go hence: when he shall let *you* go, he shall surely thrust you out hence altogether.

Exodus 11:9 <u>And the LORD said unto Moses,</u> Pharaoh shall not hearken unto you; that my wonders may be multiplied in the land of Egypt.

Exodus 12:43 <u>And the LORD said unto Moses and Aaron,</u> This *is* the ordinance of the passover: There shall no stranger eat thereof:

Exodus 14:15 <u>And the LORD said unto Moses,</u> Wherefore criest thou unto me? speak unto the children of Israel, that they go forward:

Exodus 14:26 <u>And the LORD said unto Moses,</u> Stretch out thine hand over the sea, that the waters may come again upon the Egyptians, upon their chariots, and upon their horsemen.

Exodus 16:28 <u>And the LORD said unto Moses,</u> How long refuse ye to keep my commandments and <u>my</u> laws?

Exodus 17:5 <u>And the LORD said unto Moses,</u> Go on before the people, and take with thee of the elders of Israel; and thy rod, wherewith thou smotest the river, take in thine hand, and go.

Exodus 17:14 <u>And the LORD said unto Moses,</u> Write this *for* a memorial in a book, and rehearse *it* in the ears of Joshua: for <u>I</u> will utterly put out the remembrance of Amalek from under heaven.

Exodus 19:9 <u>And the LORD said unto Moses,</u> Lo, <u>I</u> come unto thee in a thick cloud, that<u> the people may hear when I speak with thee</u>, and believe thee for ever. And Moses told the words of the people unto the LORD.

Exodus 19:10 <u>And the LORD said unto Moses,</u> Go unto the people, and sanctify them to day and to morrow, and let them wash their clothes,

Exodus 19:21 <u>And the LORD said unto Moses,</u> Go down, charge the people, lest they break through unto the LORD to gaze, and many of them perish.

Exodus 19:24 <u>And the LORD said unto him,</u> Away, get thee down, and thou shalt come up, thou, and Aaron with thee: but let not the priests and the people break through to come up unto the LORD, lest he break forth upon them.

Exodus 20:22 <u>And the LORD said unto Moses,</u> Thus thou shalt say unto the children of Israel, Ye have seen that <u>I</u> have talked with you from heaven.

Exodus 24:12 <u>And the LORD said unto Moses,</u> Come up to <u>me</u> into the mount, and be there: and <u>I</u> will give thee tables of stone, and a law, and commandments which <u>I</u> have written; that thou mayest teach them.

Exodus 30:34 <u>And the LORD said unto Moses,</u> Take unto thee sweet spices, stacte, and onycha, and galbanum; *these* sweet spices with pure frankincense: of each shall there be a like *weight*:

Exodus 32:7 <u>And the LORD said unto Moses,</u> Go, get thee down; for thy people, which thou broughtest out of the land of Egypt, have corrupted *themselves*:

Exodus 32:9 <u>And the LORD said unto Moses,</u> I have seen this people, and, behold, it *is* a stiffnecked people:

Exodus 32:33 <u>And the LORD said unto Moses,</u> Whosoever hath sinned against <u>me</u>, him will <u>I</u> blot out of my book.

Exodus 33:1 <u>And the LORD said unto Moses,</u> Depart, *and* go up hence, thou and the people which thou hast brought up out of the land of Egypt, unto the land which <u>I</u> sware unto Abraham, to Isaac, and to Jacob, saying, Unto thy seed will <u>I</u> give it:

Exodus 33:17 <u>And the LORD said unto Moses,</u> I will do this thing also that thou hast spoken: for thou hast found grace <u>in my sight</u>, and <u>I</u> know thee by name.

Exodus 33:21 <u>And the LORD said,</u> Behold, *there is* a place by me, and thou shalt stand upon a rock:

Exodus 34:1 <u>And the LORD said unto Moses,</u> Hew thee two tables of stone like unto the first: and <u>I</u> will write upon *these* tables the words that were in the first tables, which thou brakest.

Exodus 34:27 <u>And the LORD said unto Moses,</u> Write thou these words: for after the tenor of these words <u>I</u> have made a covenant with thee and with Israel.

Leviticus 16:2 <u>And the LORD said unto Moses,</u> Speak unto Aaron thy brother, that he come not at all times into the holy *place* within the vail before the mercy seat, which *is* upon the ark; that he die not: for <u>I</u> will appear in the cloud upon the mercy seat.

Leviticus 21:1 <u>And the LORD said unto Moses,</u> Speak unto the priests the sons of Aaron, and say unto them, There shall none be defiled for the dead among his people:

Numbers 3:40 <u>And the LORD said unto Moses,</u> Number all the firstborn of the males of the children of Israel from a month old and upward, and take the number of their names.

Numbers 7:11 <u>And the LORD said unto Moses,</u> They shall offer their offering, each prince on his day, for the dedicating of the altar.

Numbers 10:29 And Moses said unto Hobab, the son of Raguel the Midianite, Moses' father in law, We are journeying unto the place of which <u>the LORD said,</u> I will give it you: come thou with us, and we will do thee good: for <u>the LORD hath spoken</u> good concerning Israel.

Numbers 11:16 <u>And the LORD said unto Moses,</u> Gather unto me seventy men of the elders of Israel, whom thou knowest to be the elders of the people, and officers over them; and bring them unto the tabernacle of the congregation, that they may stand there with thee.

Numbers 11:23 And the LORD said unto Moses, Is the LORD'S hand waxed short? thou shalt see now whether my word shall come to pass unto thee or not.

Numbers 12:14 And the LORD said unto Moses, If her father had but spit in her face, should she not be ashamed seven days? let her be shut out from the camp seven days, and after that let her be received in *again*.

Numbers 14:11 And the LORD said unto Moses, How long will this people provoke me? and how long will it be ere they believe me, for all the signs which I have shewed among them?

Numbers 14:20 And the LORD said, I have pardoned according to thy word:

Numbers 15:35 <u>And the LORD said unto Moses,</u> The man shall be surely put to death: all the congregation shall stone him with stones without the camp.

Numbers 16:40 *To be* a memorial unto the children of Israel, that no stranger, which *is* not of the seed of Aaron, come near to offer incense before the LORD; that he be not as Korah, and as his company: <u>as the LORD said to him</u> by the hand of Moses.

Numbers 17:10 <u>And the LORD said unto Moses,</u> Bring Aaron's rod again before the testimony, to be kept for a token against the rebels; and thou shalt quite take away their murmurings from me, that they die not.

Numbers 18:1 And the LORD said unto Aaron, Thou and thy sons and thy father's house with thee shall bear the iniquity of the sanctuary: and thou and thy sons with thee shall bear the iniquity of your priesthood.

Numbers 21:8 And the LORD said unto Moses, Make thee a fiery serpent, and set it upon a pole: and it shall come to pass, that every one that is bitten, when he looketh upon it, shall live.

Numbers 21:34 And the LORD said unto Moses, Fear him not: for I have delivered him into thy hand, and all his people, and his land; and thou shalt do to him as thou didst unto Sihon king of the Amorites, which dwelt at Heshbon.

Numbers 22:32 And the <u>angel</u> of the LORD <u>said</u> unto him, Wherefore hast thou smitten thine ass these three times? behold, I went out to withstand thee, because *thy* way is perverse before me:

Numbers 22:35 And the <u>angel</u> of the LORD <u>said</u> unto Balaam, Go with the men: but only the word that I shall speak unto thee, that thou shalt speak. So Balaam went with the princes of Balak.

Numbers 25:4 <u>And the LORD said unto Moses,</u> Take all the heads of the people, and hang them up before the LORD against the sun, that the fierce anger of the LORD may be turned away from Israel.

Numbers 27:12 <u>And the LORD said unto Moses,</u> Get thee up into this mount Abarim, and see the land which I have given unto the children of Israel.

Numbers 27:18 <u>And the LORD said unto Moses,</u> Take thee Joshua the son of Nun, a man in whom *is* the spirit, and lay thine hand upon him;

Deuteronomy 1:42 <u>And the LORD said unto me,</u> Say unto them, Go not up, neither fight; for I *am* not among you; lest ye be smitten before your enemies.

Deuteronomy 2:9 <u>And the LORD said unto me,</u> Distress not the Moabites, neither contend with them in battle: for I will not give thee of their land *for* a possession; because I have given Ar unto the children of Lot *for* a possession.

Deuteronomy 2:31 <u>And the LORD said unto me,</u> Behold, I have begun to give Sihon and his land before thee: begin to possess, that thou mayest inherit his land.

Deuteronomy 3:2 <u>And the LORD said unto me,</u> Fear him not: for <u>I</u> will deliver him, and all his people, and his land, into thy hand; and thou shalt do unto him as thou didst unto Sihon king of the Amorites, which dwelt at Heshbon.

Deuteronomy 3:26 But the LORD was wroth with me for your sakes, and would not hear me: <u>and the LORD said unto me,</u> Let it suffice thee; speak no more unto me of this matter.

Deuteronomy 4:10 *Specially* the day that thou stoodest before the LORD thy God in Horeb, when the <u>LORD said unto me,</u> Gather me the people together, and I will make them hear my words, that they may learn to fear me all the days that they shall live upon the earth, and *that* they may teach their children.

Deuteronomy 5:28 <u>And the LORD heard</u> the voice of your words, when ye spake unto me; <u>and the LORD said unto me,</u> I have <u>heard</u> the voice of the words of this people, which they have spoken unto thee: they have well said all that they have spoken.

Deuteronomy 9:12 <u>And the LORD said unto me,</u> Arise, get thee down quickly from hence; for thy people which thou hast brought forth out of Egypt have corrupted *themselves*; they are quickly turned aside out of the way which <u>I</u> commanded them; they have made them a molten image.

Deuteronomy 10:1 <u>At that time the LORD said unto me,</u> Hew thee two tables of stone like unto the first, and come up unto me into the mount, and make thee an ark of wood.

Deuteronomy 10:11 <u>And the LORD said unto me,</u> Arise, take *thy* journey before the people, that they may go in and possess the land, which <u>I</u> sware unto their fathers to give unto them.

Deuteronomy 18:17 <u>And the LORD said unto me,</u> They have well *spoken that*which they have spoken.

Deuteronomy 31:14 <u>And the LORD said unto Moses,</u> Behold, thy days approach that thou must die: call Joshua, and present yourselves in the tabernacle of the congregation, that <u>I</u> may give him a charge. And Moses and Joshua went, and presented themselves in the tabernacle of the congregation.

Deuteronomy 31:16 <u>And the LORD said unto Moses,</u> Behold, thou shalt sleep with thy fathers; and this people will rise up, and go a whoring after the gods of the strangers of the land, whither they go *to be* among them, and will forsake me, and break my covenant which <u>I</u> have made with them.

Deuteronomy 34:4 <u>And the LORD said unto him,</u> This *is* the land which I sware unto Abraham, unto Isaac, and unto Jacob, saying, <u>I</u> will give it unto thy seed: <u>I</u> have caused thee to see *it* with thine eyes, but thou shalt not go over thither.

Joshua 3:7 <u>And the LORD said unto Joshua,</u> This day will <u>I</u> begin to magnify thee in the sight of all Israel, that they may know that, as <u>I</u> was with Moses, *so* <u>I</u> will be with thee.

Joshua 5:2 <u>At that time the LORD said unto Joshua,</u> Make thee sharp knives, and circumcise again the children of Israel the second time.

Joshua 5:9 <u>And the LORD said unto Joshua,</u> This day have <u>I</u> rolled away the reproach of Egypt from off you. Wherefore the name of the place is called Gilgal unto this day.

Joshua 6:2 And the LORD said unto Joshua, See, I have given into thine hand Jericho, and the king thereof, *and* the mighty men of valour.

Joshua 7:10 And the LORD said unto Joshua, Get thee up; wherefore liest thou thus upon thy face?

Joshua 8:1 And the LORD said unto Joshua, Fear not, neither be thou dismayed: take all the people of war with thee, and arise, go up to Ai: see, I have given into thy hand the king of Ai, and his people, and his city, and his land:

Joshua 8:18 And the LORD said unto Joshua, Stretch out the spear that *is* in thy hand toward Ai; for I will give it into thine hand. And Joshua stretched out the spear that *he had* in his hand toward the city.

Joshua 10:8 <u>And the LORD said unto Joshua,</u> Fear them not: for <u>I</u> have delivered them into thine hand; there shall not a man of them stand before thee.

Joshua 11:6 <u>And the LORD said unto Joshua,</u> Be not afraid because of them: for to morrow about this time will <u>I</u> deliver them up all slain before Israel: thou shalt hough their horses, and burn their chariots with fire.

Joshua 11:23 So Joshua took the whole land, according to all that <u>the LORD said unto Moses;</u> and Joshua gave it for an inheritance unto Israel according to their divisions by their tribes. And the land rested from war.

Joshua 13:1 Now Joshua was old *and* stricken in years; <u>and the LORD said unto him,</u> Thou art old *and* stricken in years, and there remaineth yet very much land to be possessed.

Joshua 14:6 Then the children of Judah came unto Joshua in Gilgal: and Caleb the son of Jephunneh the Kenezite said unto him, Thou knowest the thing that the <u>LORD said unto Moses</u> the man of God concerning me and thee in Kadeshbarnea.

Joshua 14:12 Now therefore give me this mountain, <u>whereof the LORD spake in that day;</u> for thou heardest in that day how the Anakims were there, and that the cities were great and fenced: if so be the LORD will be with me, then <u>I</u> shall be able to drive them out, <u>as the LORD said.</u>

Judges 1:2 <u>And the LORD said,</u> Judah shall go up: behold, <u>I</u> have delivered the land into his hand.

Judges 6:16 <u>And the LORD said unto him,</u> Surely <u>I</u> will be with thee, and thou shalt smite the Midianites as one man.

Judges 6:23 <u>And the LORD said unto him,</u> Peace *be* unto thee; fear not: thou shalt not die.

Judges 6:25 And it came to pass the same night, that <u>the LORD said unto him,</u> Take thy father's young bullock, even the second bullock of seven years old, and throw down the altar of Baal that thy father hath, and cut down the grove that *is*by it:

Judges 7:2 <u>And the LORD said unto Gideon,</u> The people that *are* with thee *are* too many for me to give the Midianites into their hands, lest Israel vaunt themselves against me, saying, Mine own hand hath saved me.

Judges 7:4 <u>And the LORD said unto Gideon,</u> The people *are* yet *too* many; bring them down unto the water, and <u>I</u> will try them for thee there: and it shall be, *that* of whom <u>I</u> say unto thee, This shall go with thee, the same shall go with thee; and of whomsoever I say unto thee, This shall not go with thee, the same shall not go.

Judges 7:5 So he brought down the people unto the water: <u>and the LORD said unto Gideon,</u> Every one that lappeth of the water with his tongue, as a dog lappeth, him shalt thou set by himself; likewise every one that boweth down upon his knees to drink.

Judges 7:7 <u>And the LORD said unto Gideon,</u> By the three hundred men that lapped will <u>I</u> save you, and deliver the Midianites into thine hand: and let all the *other* people go every man unto his place.

Judges 7:9 And it came to pass the same night, that <u>the LORD said unto him,</u> Arise, get thee down unto the host; for <u>I</u> have delivered it into thine hand.

Judges 10:11 <u>And the LORD said unto the children of Israel,</u> *Did* not <u>I</u> *deliver you* from the Egyptians, and from the Amorites, from the children of Ammon, and from the Philistines?

Judges 13:13 And the <u>angel</u> of the LORD <u>said</u> unto Manoah, Of all that I said unto the woman let her beware.

Judges 13:16 And the <u>angel</u> of the LORD <u>said</u> unto Manoah, Though thou detain me, I will not eat of thy bread: and if thou wilt offer a burnt offering, thou must offer it unto the LORD. For Manoah knew not that he *was* an angel of the LORD.

Judges 13:18 And the <u>angel</u> of the LORD <u>said</u> unto him, Why askest thou thus after my name, seeing it *is* secret?

Judges 20:18 And the children of Israel arose, and went up to the house of God, and asked counsel of God, and said, Which of us shall go up first to the battle against the children of Benjamin? <u>And the LORD said, Judah *shall go up*first.</u>

Judges 20:23 (And the children of Israel went up and wept before the LORD until even, and asked counsel of the LORD, saying, Shall I go up again to battle against the children of Benjamin my brother? <u>And the LORD said, Go up against him.</u>)

Judges 20:28 And Phinehas, the son of Eleazar, the son of Aaron, stood before it in those days,) saying, Shall I yet again go out to battle against the children of Benjamin my brother, or shall I cease? <u>And the LORD said, Go up; for to morrow I will deliver them into thine hand.</u>

1 Samuel 3:11 <u>And the LORD said to Samuel,</u> Behold, <u>I</u> will do a thing in Israel, at which both the ears of every one that heareth it shall tingle.

1 Samuel 5:2 Also in time past, when Saul was king over us, thou wast he that leddest out and broughtest in Israel: <u>and the LORD said to thee,</u> Thou shalt feed my people Israel, and thou shalt be a captain over Israel.

1 Samuel 8:7 <u>And the LORD said unto Samuel</u>, Hearken unto the voice of the people in all that they say unto thee: for they have not rejected thee, but they have rejected <u>me</u>, that <u>I</u> should not reign over them.

1 Samuel 8:22 <u>And the LORD said to Samuel,</u> Hearken unto their voice, and make them a king. And Samuel said unto the men of Israel, Go ye every man unto his city.

1 Samuel 9:17 And when Samuel saw Saul, <u>the LORD said unto him,</u> Behold the man whom <u>I spake to thee</u> of! this same shall reign over my people.

1 Samuel 16:1 <u>And the LORD said</u> <u>unto Samuel,</u> How long wilt thou mourn for Saul, seeing I have rejected him from reigning over Israel? fill thine horn with oil, and go, <u>I</u> will send thee to Jesse the Bethlehemite: for <u>I</u> have provided me a king among his sons.

1 Samuel 16:2 And Samuel said, How can I go? if Saul hear *it*, he will kill me. <u>And</u> <u>the LORD said,</u> Take an heifer with thee, and say, I am come to sacrifice to the LORD.

1 Samuel 16:7 <u>But the LORD said unto</u> <u>Samuel,</u> Look not on his countenance, or on the height of his stature; because I have refused him: for *the LORD seeth*not as man seeth; for man looketh on the outward appearance, but the LORD looketh on the heart.

1 Samuel 16:12 And he sent, and brought him in. Now he *was* ruddy, *and*withal of a beautiful countenance, and goodly to look to. <u>And the LORD said, Arise, anoint him:</u> for this *is* he.

1 Samuel 23:2 Therefore David enquired of the LORD, saying, Shall I go and smite these Philistines? <u>And the LORD said unto David,</u> Go, and smite the Philistines, and save Keilah.

1 Samuel 23:11 Will the men of Keilah deliver me up into his hand? will Saul come down, as thy servant hath heard? O LORD God of Israel, I beseech thee, tell thy servant. <u>And the LORD said,</u> He will come down.

1 Samuel 23:12 Then said David, Will the men of Keilah deliver me and my men into the hand of Saul? <u>And the LORD said,</u> They will deliver *thee* up.

1 Samuel 24:4 And the men of David said unto him, Behold the day of which <u>the LORD said</u> unto thee, Behold, I will deliver thine enemy into thine hand, that thou mayest do to him as it shall seem good unto thee. Then David arose, and cut off the skirt of Saul's robe privily.

2 Samuel 2:1 And it came to pass after this, that David enquired of the LORD, saying, Shall I go up into any of the cities of Judah? <u>And the LORD said unto him,</u> Go up. And David said, Whither shall I go up? And he said, Unto Hebron.

2 Samuel 5:19 And David enquired of the LORD, saying, Shall I go up to the Philistines? wilt thou deliver them into mine hand? <u>And the LORD said unto David</u>, Go up: for I will doubtless deliver the Philistines into thine hand.

1 Kings 8:12 Then spake Solomon, <u>The LORD said</u> that he would dwell in the thick darkness.

1 Kings 8:18 <u>And the LORD said unto David my father,</u> Whereas it was in thine heart to build an house unto my name, thou didst well that it was in thine heart.

1 Kings 9:3 <u>And the LORD said unto him,</u> I have heard thy prayer and thy supplication, that thou hast made before me: I have hallowed this house, which thou hast built, to put my name there for ever; and mine eyes and mine heart shall be there perpetually.

1 Kings 11:2 Of the nations *concerning* which <u>the LORD said unto the children of Israel,</u> Ye shall not go in to them, neither shall they come in unto you: *for* surely they will turn away your heart after their gods: Solomon clave unto these in love.

1 Kings 11:11 <u>Wherefore the LORD said unto Solomon,</u> Forasmuch as this is done of thee, and thou hast not kept <u>my</u> covenant and <u>my</u> statutes, which <u>I</u> have commanded thee, <u>I</u> will surely rend the kingdom from thee, and will give it to thy servant.

1 Kings 14:5 <u>And the LORD said unto Ahijah,</u> Behold, the wife of Jeroboam cometh to ask a thing of thee for her son; for he *is* sick: thus and thus shalt thou say unto her: for it shall be, when she cometh in, that she shall feign herself *to be* another *woman*.

1 Kings 19:15 <u>And the LORD said unto him,</u> Go, return on thy way to the wilderness of Damascus: and when thou comest, anoint Hazael *to be* king over Syria:

1 Kings 22:17 And he said, I saw all Israel scattered upon the hills, as sheep that have not a shepherd: <u>and the LORD said.</u>These have no master: let them return every man to his house in peace.

1 Kings 22:20 <u>And the LORD said,</u> Who shall persuade Ahab, that he may go up and fall at Ramothgilead? And one said on this manner, and another said on that manner.

1 Kings 22:22 <u>And the LORD said unto him,</u> Wherewith? And he said, I will go forth, and I will be a lying spirit in the mouth of all his prophets. And he said, Thou shalt persuade *him*, and prevail also: go forth, and do so.

2 Kings 1:3 But the <u>angel</u> of the LORD <u>said</u> to Elijah the Tishbite, Arise, go up to meet the messengers of the king of Samaria, and say unto them, *Is it* not because *there is* not a God in Israel, *that* ye go to enquire of Baalzebub the god of Ekron?

2 Kings 1:15 And the <u>angel</u> of the LORD <u>said</u> unto Elijah, Go down with him: be not afraid of him. And he arose, and went down with him unto the king.

2 Kings 10:30 <u>And the LORD said unto Jehu,</u> Because thou hast done well in executing *that which is* right in mine eyes, *and* hast done unto the house of Ahab according to all that *was* in mine heart, thy children of the fourth generation shall sit on the throne of Israel.

2 Kings 14:27 <u>And the LORD said</u> not that he would blot out the name of Israel from under heaven: but he saved them by the hand of Jeroboam the son of Joash.

2 Kings 18:25 Am I now come up without the LORD against this place to destroy it? <u>The LORD said to me,</u> Go up against this land, and destroy it.

2 Kings 21:4 And he built altars in the house of the LORD, of which <u>the LORD said,</u> In Jerusalem will <u>I</u> put my name.

2 Kings 21:7 And he set a graven image of the grove that he had made in the house, of which <u>the LORD said to David,</u> and to Solomon his son, In this house, and in Jerusalem, which I have chosen out of all tribes of Israel, will I put my name for ever:

2 Kings 23:27 <u>And the LORD said</u>, I will remove Judah also out of <u>my</u> <u>sight,</u> as I have removed Israel, and will cast off this city Jerusalem which I have chosen, and the house of which I said, <u>My</u> name shall be there.

1 Chronicles 14:10 And David enquired of God, saying, Shall I go up against the Philistines? and wilt thou deliver them into mine hand? <u>And the LORD said unto</u> <u>him</u>, Go up; for I will deliver them into thine hand.

2 Chronicles 6:8 <u>But the LORD said to</u> <u>David my father,</u> Forasmuch as it was in thine heart to build an house for my name, thou didst well in that it was in thine heart:

2 Chronicles 18:16 Then he said, I did see all Israel scattered upon the mountains, as sheep that have no shepherd: <u>and the LORD said,</u> These have no master; let them return *therefore* every man to his house in peace.

2 Chronicles 18:19 <u>And the LORD said,</u> Who shall entice Ahab king of Israel, that he may go up and fall at Ramothgilead? And one spake saying after this manner, and another saying after that manner.

2 Chronicles 18:20 Then there came out a spirit, and stood before the LORD, and said, I will entice him. <u>And the LORD said unto him, Wherewith?</u>

Job 1:7 <u>And the LORD said unto Satan,</u> Whence comest thou? Then Satan answered the LORD, and said, From going to and fro in the earth, and from walking up and down in it.

Job 1:8 <u>And the LORD said unto Satan,</u> Hast thou considered my servant Job, that *there is* none like him in the earth, a perfect and an upright man, one that feareth God, and escheweth evil?

Job 1:12 <u>And the LORD said unto Satan,</u> Behold, all that he hath *is* in thy power; only upon himself put not forth thine hand. So Satan went forth from the <u>presence of the LORD.</u>

Job 2:2 <u>And the LORD said unto Satan,</u> From whence comest thou? And Satan answered the LORD, and said, From going to and fro in the earth, and from walking up and down in it.

Job 2:3 <u>And the LORD said unto Satan,</u> Hast thou considered my servant Job, that *there is* none like him in the earth, a perfect and an upright man, one that feareth God, and escheweth evil? and still he holdeth fast his integrity, although thou movedst me against him, to destroy him without cause.

Job 2:6 <u>And the LORD said unto Satan,</u> Behold, he *is* in thine hand; but save his life.

Job 42:7 And it was *so*, that after the LORD had spoken these words unto Job, the LORD said to Eliphaz the Temanite, My wrath is kindled against thee, and against thy two friends: for ye have not spoken of me *the thing that is* right, as my servant Job *hath*.

Psalms 68:22 The Lord said, I will bring again from Bashan, I will bring *my people*
 again from the depths of the sea:

Psalms 110:1 The LORD said unto my Lord, Sit thou at my right hand, until I make thine enemies thy footstool.

Isaiah 8:1 Moreover the LORD said unto me, Take thee a great roll, and write in it with a man's pen concerning Mahershalalhashbaz.

Isaiah 18:4 <u>For so the LORD said unto me, I</u> will take my rest, and <u>I</u> will consider in <u>my</u> dwelling place like a clear heat upon herbs, *and* like a cloud of dew in the heat of harvest.

Isaiah 20:3 <u>And the LORD said,</u> Like as my servant Isaiah hath walked naked and barefoot three years *for* a sign and wonder upon Egypt and upon Ethiopia;

Isaiah 21:6 <u>For thus hath the Lord said unto me,</u> Go, set a watchman, let him declare what he seeth.

Isaiah 21:16 <u>For thus hath the Lord said unto me,</u> Within a year, according to the years of an hireling, and all the glory of Kedar shall fail:

Isaiah 29:13 <u>Wherefore the Lord said,</u> Forasmuch as this people draw near *me* with their mouth, and with their lips do honour <u>me</u>, but have removed their heart far from <u>me</u>, and their fear toward <u>me</u> is taught by the precept of men:

Isaiah 36:10 And am I now come up without the LORD against this land to destroy it? <u>the LORD said unto me,</u> Go up against this land, and destroy it.

Jeremiah 1:7 <u>But the LORD said unto me,</u> Say not, I *am* a child: for thou shalt go to all that <u>I</u> shall send thee, and whatsoever <u>I</u> command thee thou shalt speak.

Jeremiah 1:9 Then <u>the LORD</u> put forth <u>his hand,</u> and <u>touched my mouth.</u> <u>And the LORD said unto me,</u> Behold, <u>I</u> have put <u>my</u> words in thy mouth.

Jeremiah 1:14 <u>Then the LORD said unto me,</u> Out of the north an evil shall break forth upon all the inhabitants of the land.

Jeremiah 3:6 <u>The LORD said also unto me</u> in the days of Josiah the king, Hast thou seen *that* which backsliding Israel hath done? she is gone up upon every high mountain and under every green tree, and there hath played the harlot.

Jeremiah 3:11 <u>And the LORD said unto me,</u> The backsliding Israel hath justified herself more than treacherous Judah.

Jeremiah 4:27 <u>For thus hath the LORD said,</u> The whole land shall be desolate; yet will <u>I</u> not make a full end.

Jeremiah 11:6 <u>Then the LORD said unto me,</u> Proclaim all these words in the cities of Judah, and in the streets of Jerusalem, saying, Hear ye the words of this covenant, and do them.

Jeremiah 11:9 <u>And the LORD said unto me,</u> A conspiracy is found among the men of Judah, and among the inhabitants of Jerusalem.

Jeremiah 13:6 And it came to pass after many days, <u>that the LORD said unto me,</u> Arise, go to Euphrates, and take the girdle from thence, which <u>I</u> commanded thee to hide there.

Jeremiah 14:14 <u>Then the LORD said unto me,</u> The prophets prophesy lies in <u>my</u> name: <u>I</u> sent them not, neither have <u>I</u> commanded them, neither spake unto them: they prophesy unto you a false vision and divination, and a thing of nought, and the deceit of their heart.

Jeremiah 15:11 <u>The LORD said,</u> Verily it shall be well with thy remnant; verily <u>I</u> will cause the enemy to entreat thee *well* in the time of evil and in the time of affliction.

Ezekiel 4:13 <u>And the LORD said,</u> Even thus shall the children of Israel eat their defiled bread among the Gentiles, whither <u>I</u> will drive them.

Ezekiel 9:4 <u>And the LORD said unto him,</u> Go through the midst of the city, through the midst of Jerusalem, and set a mark upon the foreheads of the men that sigh and that cry for all the abominations that be done in the midst thereof.

Ezekiel 23:36 <u>The LORD said moreover unto me;</u> Son of man, wilt thou judge Aholah and Aholibah? yea, declare unto them their abominations;

Ezekiel 44:5 <u>And the LORD said unto me,</u> Son of man, mark well, and behold with thine eyes, and hear with thine ears all that <u>I</u> say unto thee concerning all the ordinances of the house of the LORD, and all the laws thereof; and mark well the entering in of the house, with every going forth of the sanctuary.

Hosea 1:2 The beginning of the word of the LORD by Hosea. <u>And the LORD said to Hosea,</u> Go, take unto thee a wife of whoredoms and children of whoredoms: for the land hath committed great whoredom, *departing* from the LORD.

Hosea 1:4 <u>And the LORD said unto him,</u> Call his name Jezreel; for yet a little *while*, and <u>I</u> will avenge the blood of Jezreel upon the house of Jehu, and will cause to cease the kingdom of the house of Israel.

Amos 7:8 <u>And the LORD said unto me,</u> Amos, what seest thou? And <u>I</u> said, A plumbline. Then said the Lord, Behold, <u>I</u> will set a plumbline in the midst of my people Israel: <u>I</u> will not again pass by them any more:

Amos 7:15 And the LORD took me as I followed the flock, and <u>the LORD said unto me,</u> Go, prophesy unto <u>my</u> people Israel.

Zechariah 3:2 <u>And the LORD said unto Satan,</u> The LORD rebuke thee, O Satan; even the LORD that hath chosen Jerusalem rebuke thee: *is* not this a brand plucked out of the fire?

Zechariah 11:13 <u>And the LORD said unto me,</u> Cast it unto the potter: a goodly price that <u>I</u> was prised at of them. And I took the thirty *pieces* of silver, and cast them to the potter in the house of the LORD.

Zechariah 11:15 <u>And the LORD said unto me,</u> Take unto thee yet the instruments of a foolish shepherd.

God Has Eyes

How the Human Eye Works

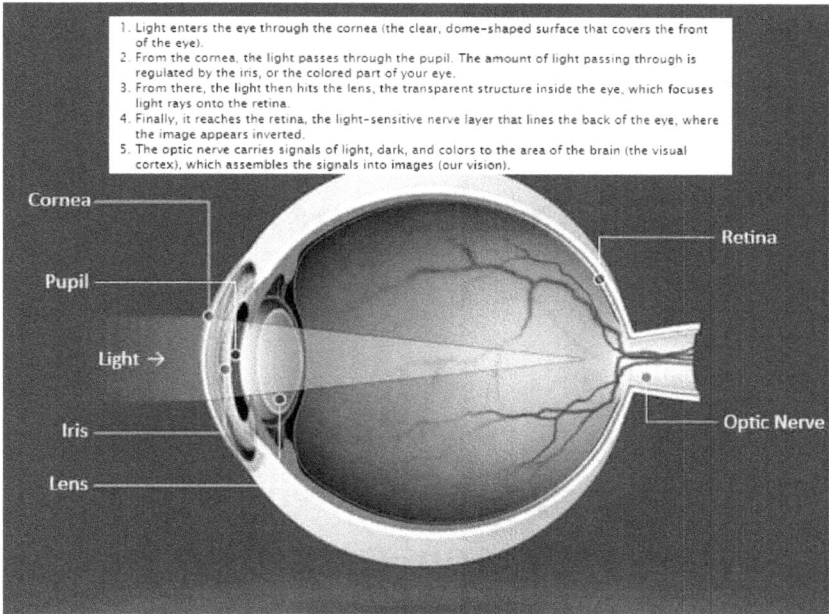

1. Light enters the eye through the cornea (the clear, dome-shaped surface that covers the front of the eye).
2. From the cornea, the light passes through the pupil. The amount of light passing through is regulated by the iris, or the colored part of your eye.
3. From there, the light then hits the lens, the transparent structure inside the eye, which focuses light rays onto the retina.
4. Finally, it reaches the retina, the light-sensitive nerve layer that lines the back of the eye, where the image appears inverted.
5. The optic nerve carries signals of light, dark, and colors to the area of the brain (the visual cortex), which assembles the signals into images (our vision).

Cornea

Pupil

Light →

Iris

Lens

Retina

Optic Nerve

English Translation of the Holy Quran
Maulana Muhammad Ali

8:22 Surely the vilest of beasts, in Allah's <u>sight</u>, are the deaf, the dumb, who understand not.

8:55 Surely the vilest of beasts in Allah's <u>sight</u> are those who disbelieve, then they would not believe.

Genesis 1:4 <u>And God saw the light,</u> that *it was* good: and God divided the light from the darkness.

Genesis 1:10 And God <u>called</u> the dry *land* Earth; and the gathering together of the waters called <u>he</u> Seas: and <u>God saw that *it* was good</u>.

Genesis 1:12 And the earth brought forth grass, *and* herb yielding seed after his kind, and the tree yielding fruit, whose seed *was* in itself, after his kind: and <u>God saw that *it was* good</u>.

Genesis 1:18 And to rule over the day and over the night, and to divide the light from the darkness: <u>and God saw that *it was* good</u>.

Genesis 1:21 And God created great whales, and every living creature that moveth, which the waters brought forth abundantly, after their kind, and every winged fowl after his kind: and <u>God saw that *it was* good</u>.

Genesis 1:25 And God made the beast of the earth after his kind, and cattle after their kind, and every thing that creepeth upon the earth after his kind: <u>and God saw that *it was* good</u>.

Genesis 1:31 <u>And God saw every thing that he had made</u>, and, behold, *it* was very good. And the evening and the morning were the sixth day.

Genesis 6:5 <u>And GOD saw that the</u> <u>wickedness of man *was* great in the earth,</u> and *that* every imagination of the thoughts of his heart *was* only evil continually.

2 Kings 4:25 So she went and came unto the man of God to mount Carmel. And it came to pass, when the man of <u>God saw her</u> <u>afar off</u>, that he said to Gehazi his servant, Behold, *yonder is* that Shunammite:

Jonah 3:10 <u>And God saw their works</u>, that they turned from their evil way; and God repented of the evil, that he had said that he would do unto them; and he did *it* not.

Proverbs 15:3 <u>The eyes of the LORD</u> are in every place, keeping watch on the evil and the good.

Genesis 29:31 <u>And when the LORD saw</u> that Leah *was* hated, he opened her womb: but Rachel *was* barren.

Exodus 3:4 <u>And when the LORD saw</u> that he turned aside to see, <u>God called</u> unto him out of the midst of the bush, and said, Moses, Moses. And he said, Here *am* I.

Deuteronomy 32:19 <u>And when the LORD saw *it*,</u> he abhorred *them*, because of the provoking of his sons, and of his daughters.

2 Kings 14:26 <u>For the LORD saw the affliction of Israel,</u> *that it was* very bitter: for *there was* not any shut up, nor any left, nor any helper for Israel.

2 Chronicles 12:7 <u>And when the LORD saw</u> that they humbled themselves, the word of the LORD came to Shemaiah, saying, They have humbled themselves; *therefore* I will not destroy them, but I will grant them some deliverance; and my wrath shall not be poured out upon Jerusalem by the hand of Shishak.

Isaiah 59:15 Yea, truth faileth; and he *that* departeth from evil maketh himself a prey: <u>and the LORD saw *it*</u>, and it displeased him that *there was* no judgment.

GOD SITS AND LAUGHS

Psalm 2:4 (KJV)

<u>He</u> that <u>sitteth</u> in the heavens shall <u>laugh</u>: the LORD shall have them in derision.

<u>Sit</u>: Adopt or be in a position in which one's weight is supported by one's <u>buttocks</u> rather than one's feet and one's <u>back</u> is upright.

<u>Laugh</u>: make the spontaneous sounds and movements of the <u>face and body</u> that are the instinctive expressions of lively amusement and sometimes also of contempt or derision.

GOD HAS LEGS

Genesis 3:8 And they heard the voice of the LORD **God walking** in the garden in the cool of the day: and Adam and his wife hid themselves from the presence of the LORD God amongst the trees of the garden.

Genesis 5:24

King James Version

And Enoch walked with God

God in Three Persons?

The White man's Made-up Religion

God in Three Persons?

The White man's Made-up Religion

Father - Son - Ghost

(1) God is <u>a person.</u>

(2) The Son is <u>a person.</u>

(3) A ghost is <u>a person</u>.

(4) <u>All 3 are one person</u>.

The White man's math 1+1+1=1

The White man's logic: <u>Admits that God is a person</u>.

Grade level for knowing that 1+1+1=3
2nd grade

HOLY, HOLY, HOLY, LORD GOD ALMIGHTY

**Holy, holy, holy! Lord God Almighty!
Early in the morning our song shall rise to thee;
holy, holy, holy! merciful and mighty, <u>God in three
persons</u>, blessed Trinity!**

Grade level for letting yourself be tricked by the above:

Associates degree, Bachelor's degree, Master's degree, Doctor of Philosophy, Doctor of Education, Juris Doctorate (J.D.), Medical Doctor (M.D.), Doctor of Dental Surgery (D.D.S.), Doctor of Pharmacy (Pharm.D.) ect.

<u>And help for those who still believe it</u>. (Page 150)

From:

Message To The Black Man in America

By:

The Honorable Elijah Muhammad

Scan QR code to buy
扫描购买
Escanea el código para comprar

Chapter 3

Message To The Black Man

Is God a Spirit or a Man?

God is a man and we just cannot make Him other than man, lest we make him an inferior one; for man's intelligence has no equal in other than man. His wisdom is infinite; capable of accomplishing anything that his brain can conceive.

A spirit is subjected to us and not we to the spirit. Habakkuk uses the pronoun "He" in reference to God. This pronoun "He" is only used in the case when we refer to a man or boy or something of the male sex.

Are we living in a material universe or a "spirit" universe?We are material beings and live in a material universe. Would not we be making ourselves fools to be looking forward to see that which cannot be seen, only felt?

Where is our proof for such a God (spirit) to teach that God is other than man?It is due to your ignorance of God, or you are one deceived by the devil whose nature is to mislead you in the knowledge of God.

You originally came from the God of Righteousness and have the opportunity to return, while the devils are from the man devil (Yakub), who has ruled the world for the past 6,000 years under falsehood, labeled under the name of God and His prophets.

The worst thing to ever happen to the devils is: the truth of them made manifest that they are really the devils whom the righteous (all members of the black nation) should shun and never accept as truthful guides of God!

This is why the devils have always persecuted and killed the righteous. But the time has at last arrived that Allah (God) will put an end to their persecuting and killing the righteous (the black nation).

GOD IS A MAN

I and my followers have been suffering cruel persecution - police brutality for the past 34 years; but have patience, my dear followers, for release is in sight. Even those who made mockery of you shall be paid fully for his or her mockery; for the prophesy of Habakkuk is true if understood; wherein he says, "Thou wentest forth for the salvation of Thy people" (the so-called Negroes) 3:13.

Never before this time did anyone come for the salvation of the so-called Negroes in America, whose rights have been ignored by their enemies (the white race) for 400 years. Now it is incumbent upon Allah to defend the rights of his lost-found helpless people, called Negroes by their enemies.

The whole of the third chapter of
Habukkuk is devoted to the coming and work
of God against our enemies and our
deliverance. We must not take our enemies
for our spiritual guides lest we regret it. You
are already deceived by them.

Why seek to follow them and their evil
doings? If I would say that God is not man, I
would be a liar before him and stand to be
condemned. Remember! You look forward to
seeing God or the coming of the "Son of
Man" (a man from a man) and not the coming
of a "spirit." Let that one among you who
believes God is other than man prove it.!

Chapter 4

Message To The Black Man

The Coming of God: Is He Man or Spirit?

According to the dictionary of the Bible: Teman, a son of Esau by Adah (Gen. 36:11, 15, 42) and in I Chron. 1:36, now if Habakkuk saw God come or coming from the sons of Esau (Eliphaz), then God must be a man and not a spook.

If Habakkuk's (3:3) prophecy refers to some country, town, or city, if there be any truth at all in this prophecy, then we can say that this prophet saw God as a material being, belonging to the human family of the earth-and not to a spirit (ghost).

In the same chapter and verse, Habakkuk saw the Holy One from Mount Paran. This is also earthly, somewhere in Arabia. Here the Bible makes a difference between God and another person who is called the Holy One. Which one should we take for our God? For one is called God, while another One is called Holy One.

The Holy One: His glory covered the heavens and the earth was full of His praise. It has been a long time since the earth was full of praise for a Holy One. Even to this hour, the people do not care for Holy People and will persecute and kill the Holy One, if God does not intervene.

In the fourth verse of the above chapter, it says, "He had horns coming out of his hands: and there was the hiding of His power." Such science to represent the God's power could confuse the ignorant masses of the world. Two gods are here represented at the same time. (It is good that God makes Himself manifest to the ignorant world today.)

"The burning coals, went forth at His feet," has a meaning but what is the meaning? The ignorant do not know. "The burning coals" could refer to the anger and war among the people where His foot trod within the borders of the wicked. (Here God has feet--Spirits do not have feet and hands.)

This Holy One does not refer to anyone of the past- not Moses, Jesus or Mohammed of the past 1300 years. "For this Holy One the perpetual hills did bow. Cushan in affliction; the curtains of the land of Midian did tremble." (What is meant by the curtains trembling?) (Who is Cushan?) "The mountains saw thee, they trembled. (What does this mean?) "The sun and moon stood still in their habitation." (What does this mean?)

The answers to the above questions are easy when we understand who this God called the Holy One coming from Mount Paran is. The 13th verse should clear the way for such undertaking; for it tells us why all these great things took place on the coming of the Holy One from Mount Paran.

It says: "Thou wentest forth for the salvation of thy people (not for all people) for the salvation with thine anointed (His Apostle). He wounded the head out of the house of the wicked by discovering the foundation unto the neck (by exposing the truth and ruling powers of the wicked race of devils,)"

"Cushan" represents the Black Nation which is afflicted by the white race."The curtains of the land of Midian" could mean the falsehood spread over the people by the white race and their leaders trembling from being exposed by the truth.

"The mountains" represent the great, rich and powerful political men of the wicked; they also are trembling and being divided and scattered over the earth. "The Holy One" is God in person and not a spirit!

The Honorable Elijah Muhammad

"I can show you my God - show me yours."

The belief in a God other than man (a spirit) Allah has taught me goes back into the millions of years--long before Yakub (the father of the devils) because the knowledge of God was kept as a secret from the public.

This is the first time that it has ever been revealed, and we, the poor rejected and despised people, are blessed to be the first of all the people of earth to receive this secret knowledge of God.

If this people (the white race) would teach you truth which has been revealed to me, they would be hastening their own doom, for they were not created to teach us the truth but rather to teach us falsehood (just contrary to the truth).

God Has Human Emotions

God gets Jealous, Loves and Hates

Joshua 24:19 King James Version

And Joshua said unto the people, Ye cannot serve the LORD: for he is an holy God; <u>he is a jealous God</u>; he will not forgive your transgressions nor your sins.

Exodus 20:5 King James Version

Thou shalt not bow down thyself to them, nor serve them:<u> for I the LORD thy God am a jealous God</u>, visiting the iniquity of the fathers upon the children unto the third and fourth generation of them that hate me;

Malachi 1 King James Version

The burden of the word of the LORD to Israel by Malachi. <u>I have loved you, saith the LORD</u>. Yet ye say, Wherein hast thou loved us? Was not Esau Jacob's brother? saith the LORD: yet I loved Jacob, And I hated Esau, and laid his mountains and his heritage waste for the dragons of the wilderness.

Grade level for knowing that a ghost can't get jealous:
2nd grade

Grade level for knowing that a ghost can't Love or Hate:
2nd grade

God Has A Brain, He Thinks!

Jeremiah 29:11-1

King James Version

For I know the <u>thoughts</u> that <u>I think</u> toward you,<u> saith the LORD</u>, thoughts of peace, and not of evil, to give you an expected end. Then shall ye call upon <u>me</u>, and ye shall go and pray unto <u>me</u>, and <u>I</u> will hearken unto you. And ye shall seek <u>me</u>, and find <u>me</u>, when ye shall search for me with all your heart.

**Grade level for knowing that you need a brain in order to think with:
2nd grade**

Proverbs 2:6

For the LORD giveth <u>wisdom</u>:
<u>out of his mouth</u> cometh <u>knowledge</u> and
<u>understanding</u>.

<u>Wisdom</u>
You must have a brain in order to have
wisdom.

<u>Mouth</u>
You need a head to have a mouth.

<u>Knowledge</u>
You must have a brain to have
knowledge and understanding.

Deuteronomy 5:28

<u>And the L</u>ORD <u>heard the voice </u>of your words, when ye spake unto me; <u>and the L</u>ORD <u>said unto me</u>, <u>I</u> have <u>heard</u> the voice of the words of this people, which they have spoken unto thee: they have well said all that they have spoken.

(The **God** of the Bible gets angry, has regrets, gets lonely, loves, has loyalties, is jealous, feels compassion, and is vindictive. God is a man, not a spirit!)

In The Holy Quran
God is a Person

Escanee el código QR para leer el Sagrado Corán

Scan QR code to read the Holy Quran

扫描阅读古兰经

Holy Quran 55:27

And there endures forever the person of thy Lord, the Lord of glory and honour.

112:1 Say: <u>He</u>, Allah, is One.

112:2 Allah is <u>He</u> on Whom all depend.

112:3 <u>He</u> begets not, nor is <u>He</u> begotten;

112:4 And none is like <u>Him</u>.

31:1 <u>I</u>, Allah, am the Best <u>Knower</u>.

I - Personal Pronoun

He - Personal Pronoun

Him - Personal Pronoun

Knower - You need a brain to be a knower.

31:34 Surely Allah is <u>He</u> with Whom is the <u>knowledge</u> of the Hour, and <u>He</u> sends down the rain, and <u>He</u> <u>knows</u> what is in the wombs. And no one knows what he will earn on the morrow. And no one knows in what land he will die. Surely <u>Allah is Knowing, Aware</u>.

Allah (God) Has a Conversation With His Angels Holy Quran 2:30

2:30 And when thy <u>Lord said</u> to the angels, <u>I</u> am going to place a ruler in the earth, <u>they said</u>: Wilt Thou place in it such as make mischief in it and shed blood? And we celebrate Thy praise and extol Thy holiness. <u>He said:</u> Surely <u>I</u> <u>know</u> what you know not.

Conversation definition:

A talk, especially an informal one, <u>between two or more PEOPLE,</u> in which news and ideas are exchanged.

Grade level for knowing that ghost can't have a conversation:
2nd grade

2:41 And believe in that which <u>I</u> have revealed, verifying that which is with you, and be not the first to deny it; neither take a mean price for <u>My</u> messages; and keep your duty to <u>Me</u>, <u>Me</u> alone.

Allah (God) Speaks in the 1st Person

2:1 I, Allah, am the best Knower.

2:2 This Book, there is <u>no doubt</u> in it, is a guide to those who keep their duty,

Meaning of the first person in English:

(1) Showing that <u>someone </u>is speaking **or** writing about <u>themselves</u>.

(2) The form of a verb or pronoun that is used when <u>people</u> are speaking or writing about <u>themselves</u>.

Definition of reality

(1) The quality or state of <u>being real</u>.

(2) The state or quality of <u>having existence</u> or substance.

The Holy Quran says Allah is the ONLY reality.

In the Yusuf Ali Translation of The Qur'an, Chapter 31 Luqman, the 30th verse, Yusuf Ali translates: "That is because <u>Allah is The (only) Reality,</u> and because whatever else they invoke besides Allah is Falsehood; And because <u>Allah—He</u> is The Most High, Most Great."

The Three States of Matter

Matter can <u>only</u> exist in one of three main states: solid, liquid, or gas.

<u>Question</u>: What state of matter is the holy ghost God in?

Below is a children's video link for Black Pastors who don't understand the three states of matter.

Scan QR code to play video

掃描代碼以播放視頻

Escanea el código para reproducir el video.

The Three States of Matter

(1) Solid matter is composed of tightly packed particles. A solid will retain its shape; the particles are not free to move around.

(2) Liquid matter is made of more loosely packed particles. It will take the shape of its container. Particles can move about within a liquid, but they are packed densely enough that volume is maintained.

(3) Gaseous matter is composed of particles packed so loosely that it has neither a defined shape nor a defined volume. A gas can be compressed.

Still Not Convinced?

**You Tube Video by
The Honorable Minister Louis Farrakhan**

**"Master Fard Muhammad:
The Man And What He Revealed"
(Start video at 47:20)**

Scan QR code to play video

Escanea el código para reproducir el video.

掃描代碼以播放視頻

The Honorable Minister Louis Farrakhan

Who is God; Saviours' Day '91

(Start video at 46:35)

Scan QR code to play video

Escanea el código para reproducir el video.

掃描代碼以播放視頻

Saviours' Day 1971 by The Honorable Elijah Muhammad

"I can show you my God - show me yours."

(Start video at 23:00)

Scan QR code to play video

Escanea el código para reproducir el video.

掃描代碼以播放視頻

For Clergy who refuse to leave the Slave master's religion(who went to school on the "short-bus") and continue to count three persons (including a ghost) as one person, please view the video below on how to count and then read page 150.

Scan QR code to play video

Escanea el código para reproducir el video.

掃描代碼以播放視頻

The National Institute of <u>Mental</u>
<u>Health</u> Information Resource Center
Available in English and Español
Hours: 8:30 a.m. to 5 p.m.
Phone: 1-866-615-6464
TTY: 1-301-443-8431
TTY (toll-free): 1-866-415-8051
Email: <u>nimhinfo@nih.gov</u>
Fax: 1-301-443-4279
Mail: National Institute of Mental Health Office
of Science Policy, Planning, and
Communications
6001 Executive Boulevard, Room 6200, MSC
9663
Bethesda, MD 20892-9663

Scan QR Code to Buy
Escanea el código para comprar

扫描购买

If this book has helped you in any way and you feel that it is good for the Black man and woman. Help me to continue spreading the word. Make a donation!

Scan QR code to make a donation
Escanee el código QR para hacer una donación

请捐款

Isaiah 55:8-9 (KJV)

For <u>my thoughts</u> are not your thoughts, neither are your ways <u>my</u> ways, <u>saith the LORD</u>. For as the heavens are higher than the earth, so are <u>my</u> ways higher than your ways, and <u>my</u> <u>thoughts</u> than your thoughts.

God thinks - God talks
God uses personal pronouns.
GOD IS A MAN!

The Trinity Explained

"God in three persons"

God #1 (The Father) = Is a person

God #2 (The Son) = Is a person

God #3 (The Holy Ghost) = Is a person

All three separate persons

are actually one person.

The math that they want you to believe.

$$1+1+1=1$$

The math that a 2 yr old child believes.

$$1+1+1=3$$

Which one do you believe?

What is the definition of a person?

CAN THE DEVIL FOOL A MUSLIM?
-NOT NOWADAYS-

John 4:24 (KJV)

God is a Spirit: and they that worship <u>him</u> must worship <u>him</u> in spirit and in truth.

Notice the total contradiction of this verse, it would fool the average Negro. God is a spirit but at the same time, the <u>personal</u> pronoun "<u>HIM</u>" is used twice to refer to God. Thats why in the front of every Bible (KJV) there is a disclaimer warning that the Bible is revised from the original.

Revised:
To <u>alter something</u> already written or printed.

From chapter 1 - Message To The Black Man - Who is that Mystery God? Part I

The Christians do not believe in God as being a human being, yet they believe in Him as being the Father of all human beings. They also refer to God as He, Him, Man, King and The Ruler.

They teach that God sees, hears, talks, walks, stands, sits, rides, and flies; that He grieves or sorrows; and that He is interested in the affairs of human beings. They also teach that once upon a time He made the first man like Himself in the image and likeness of Himself, but yet they believe that He, Himself, is not a man or human.

They preach and prophesy of His coming and that He will be seen on the Judgment Day but is not man. They cannot tell us what He looks like, yet man is made like Him and in the image of God, and yet they still say that He is a mystery (unknown).

From chapter 2 - Message To The Black Man - Who is that Mystery God? Part II

Did God say that He was a Mystery God, or did someone say it of Him? Did God say that He was only a Spirit, or did someone say it of Him?

The most important question of all questions that one could ask is, "Who is God?" It is like a child who does not know his father asking his mother to tell him the name of his father, wanting to know what his father looks like and if he favors his father.

From chapter 5 - Message To The Black Man - The Origin of God As a Spirit and Not a Man

The belief in a God other than man (a spirit) Allah has taught me goes back into the millions of years--long before Yakub (the father of the devils) because the knowledge of God was kept as a secret from the public.

This is the first time that it has ever been revealed, and we, the poor rejected and despised people, are blessed to be the first of all the people of earth to receive this secret knowledge of God.

If this people (the white race) would teach you truth which has been revealed to me, they would be hastening their own doom, for they were not created to teach us the truth but rather to teach us falsehood (just contrary to the truth).

In The Bible (KJV) and Holy Quran, God is a living breathing person.

living
(adjective)

The definition of living is <u>a person that is alive or active</u>.

An example of living is <u>a breathing person with brain activity</u>.

Living refers to any organism that shows the characteristics of <u>being alive</u>.

(The above is 3rd or 4th grade knowledge)

Different Translations
The Same Results:
God Is Alive!

The Holy Quran Surah (chapter 3)
Al-'Imran

-Maulana Muhammad Ali-

Allah, (there is) no god but <u>He, the Ever-living</u>, the <u>Self</u>-subsisting, by Whom all subsist.

-Yusuf Ali-

Allah! there is no god but <u>He the Living</u> the <u>Self</u>-Subsisting Eternal

-Muhammad Marmaduke Pickthall-

Allah! There is no God save Him, <u>the Alive</u>, the Eternal.

Jeremiah 10:10

"But the LORD *is* the true God, **he *is* the living God**, and an everlasting king: at his wrath the earth shall tremble, and the nations shall not be able to abide his indignation."

Jeremiah 10:10

"But the LORD *is* the true God, **he *is* the living God**, and an everlasting king: at his wrath the earth shall tremble, and the nations shall not be able to abide his indignation."

Psalms 42:2

"My soul thirsteth for God, **for the living God**: when shall I come and appear before God?"

Hebrews 10:31

"It is a fearful thing to fall into the hands of **the living God**."

Deuteronomy 5:26

"For who is there of all flesh who has heard the voice of **the living God** speaking from the midst of the fire, as we have, and lived?"

1 Sam 17:26

"And David spake to the men that stood by him, saying, What shall be done to the man that killeth this Philistine, and taketh away the reproach from Israel? for who is this uncircumcised Philistine, that he should defy the armies of **the living God**?"

Dan 6:20

"And when he came to the den, he cried with a lamentable voice unto Daniel: and the king spake and said to Daniel, O Daniel, **servant of the living God**, is thy God, whom thou servest continually, able to deliver thee from the lions?"

2 Corinthians 3:3

"Forasmuch as ye are manifestly declared to be the epistle of Christ ministered by us, written not with ink, but with the Spirit of **the living God**; not in tables of stone, but in fleshy tables of the heart."

Jeremiah 23:36

"And the burden of
the LORD shall ye mention no more:
for every man's word shall be his
burden; for ye have perverted the
words of **the living God**, of
the LORD of hosts our God."

1 Timothy 6:17

"Charge them that are rich in this world, that they be not highminded, nor trust in uncertain riches, but in **the living God**, who giveth us richly all things to enjoy;"

Romans 9:26

"And it shall come to pass, that in the place where it was said unto them, Ye are not my people; there shall they be called the children **of the living God**."

The Black Preacher

The Black Preacher is the worst enemy to the rise of our people. The Slave master uses them as his "foot-soldiers," to keep the lie of the "mystery holy ghost" instilled into generation after generation of our people.

The Negro Preacher is loyal to his master. Much like Samuel Jackson in "Django Unchained." He (The Negro Preacher) goes to the Slave master's Theological Seminary School to get a "stamp of approval" from him to preach the spook-God theory.

Why would anyone, after reading this book choose to remain in ignorance?

-Ernest Muhammad

**King James was a homosexual
slave master
that had Sex with his own mother.**

Scan QR code to play Video
Escanea el código para reproducir el video.

You Tube Video by Bro. Nuri Muhammad

This is the disclaimer warning that appears in every King James Version

"Translated out of the original tongues And with the former translations diligently compared and revised."

What is a version?

An account of a matter <u>from a particular person's point of view.</u>

What is revised?

To <u>alter something</u> already written or printed.

What is the origin of Father-Son-Holy Ghost?

Read this book and find out.

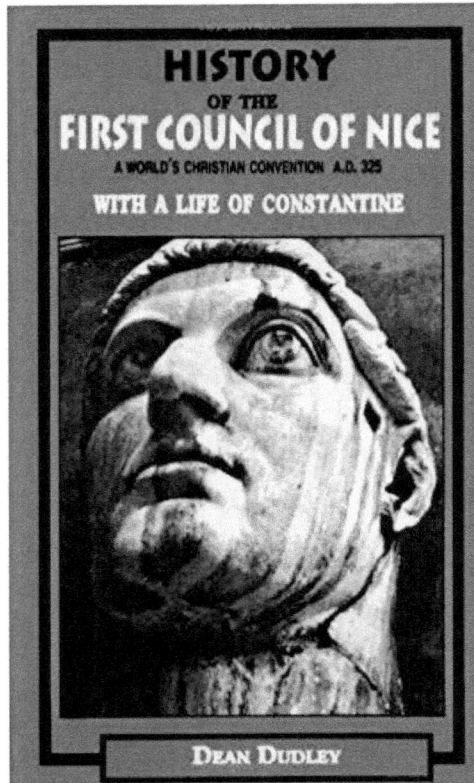

The Roman emperor Constantine the Great, while himself not really a Christian, convened and played a major role in the Council of Nicaea, <u>which laid the groundwork for acceptance of the Trinity doctrine.</u>

Christianity The Slave Making Religion

You Tube Video by:

Dr. Wesley Muhammad

Scan QR code to play video

Escanea el código para reproducir el video.

掃描代碼以播放視頻

Open Book Test

1. In order to speak, a person must have a_____.

2. In order to walk, a person must have_____.

3. In order to think, a person must have a
_____.

4. In order to sit, a person must have an_____.

5.   In order to laugh, a person must have a_____.

6.   In order to see, a person must have_____.

7. Do you still believe in ghost?

Yes_____   Hell No, My Brother!_____

**Congratulations if you got all seven correct!
You took the "Red Pill," you are now no longer a slave.
Lies from your religious leaders will no longer affect
you. Enjoy your new freedom!**

The Supreme Wisdom Lessons teach us the reason why the Devil teaches the Eighty-Five Percent about a mystery God:

To conceal the True God, which is the Son of man, and make slaves out of the 85% by keeping them worshiping something he knows they cannot see (invisible), and he lives and makes himself rich from their labor.

The 85% knows that it rains, hails and snows; also, hears it thunder above his head, but they do not try to learn who is it that causes all this to happen---by letting the 5% teach them. He believes in the 10% on face value.

If you feel that this book is the truth and good for Black folks, show some love, take a photo of the book or make a short video and put it on social media.

Master Fard Muhammad

I have proved, with the help of Allah and the teachings of the Hon. Elijah Muhammad, beyond a shadow of doubt, with actual facts, with simple 2nd grade math and common sense that God is a man.

Can you or your Pastor prove that God is a spook, spirit or ghost?

If you can, email me :

godisaman2020@gmail.com

To date, no one has answered this challenge, because you can't prove something that does not exist. You should be able to prove what you say you believe in - I did.

- Ernest Muhammad

Black folks are tired of being lied to by their religious leaders. We've been in mental slavery for a long time, but now it looks like a change is gonna come.

www.ingramcontent.com/pod-product-compliance
Lightning Source LLC
LaVergne TN
LVHW021447080426
835509LV00018B/2199